Fighting

With

HARD TIMES!

Birister Sharma

Copyright © 2022 Birister Sharma

All Rights Reserved.

Made with ❤on the Notion Press Platform

www.notionpress.com

Dedicated to my loving wife....

Pallabi Devi Sharma

I surrendered to you, O my Lord……

"Om Namah Shivaya"

One Word

Your life is a cycle of good times and bad times. Without this cycle, your life is not possible. This is the law of this world. If the good times will arrive today, the bad times will naturally follow the next day. In the similar fashion, if the bad times will strike in your life today, the good times will naturally follow the next day. This is the continuous cycle. Nobody can stop it. This is the fact. This is the part of your life. You can't deny it. And you've to accept this truth.

$$\text{Good Times} \leftrightharpoons \text{Bad Times}$$

$$\text{Bad Times} \leftrightharpoons \text{Good Times}$$

You never expect only good times in your life. If there is life, there are both good times and bad times like day and night. If this part of the beach is full of hard times, then the other part of the beach is full of good times; and vice versa. You've to cross these beaches of life all alone. You've to sail all alone. You've to swim all alone. Then only you can reach to your ultimate destination of your life.

Whenever the hard times will strike in your life, don't get scared, but face them like a brave soldier. Be positive! Believe in yourself. Fight with full might. Keep your hopes alive. Be patient! And never give up! You'll definitely come over your hard times.

‿***‿

ᔐ***ᔑ

2

"Without destruction, there is no creation.

Without hard times, there are no good times.

Without darkness, there is no brightness.

This is the universal law."

ᔐ***ᔑ

1

If there is a stormy night in your life, don't worry.

Be strong.

Be patient.

Things will get better in your life.

Nothing will remain forever.

The heavy downpour will never last forever.....

It'll end sooner or later....

Just hold your breath.

Just hold your nerve.

ↄ***ↄ

If everything in your life turns against you….

If everyone in your life turns against you…

If you feel lonely…..

If you're in deep despair and hopelessness……

Then look at the sky……

And remember that the airplane takes off against the wind….

ﮞ***ﮞ

No matter, how many obstacles knock in your life…..

No matter, how many difficulties, try to block your life….

No matter, how many problems hit in your life…..

But, never give up your persistence.

Be like a river…..

Since, a river cuts through a rock not because of its energy and power, but its continued persistence.

ↄ***ↄ

If today is hard for you,

If this week is hard for you,

If this month is hard for you,

If this year is hard for you,

If the present moment is hard for you,

These hard times will pass.

Always remember 3 words in your life 'TIME WILL PASS.'

∽***∽

How can you stay in your hard times?

You've to stay always strong in your hard times.

You've to keep your self-believe.

You've to keep your self-confidence.

You've to keep your hopes alive.

You've to keep your positive attitude.

You've to keep your enthusiasm.

You've to keep your patience.

ᵔ***ᵔ

If you want to become a tough in your life,

Then greet every tough situation of your life.

Don't try to run away from the tough situation of your life.

When the huge tide rises in the sea, then the hidden treasure of the sea,

Such as seashells, precious stones and gems will emerge out at the seashore.

In the similar way, **when the hardest time will hit in your life,**

You'll know how much inner potential do you have stored within you.

You're allowed to scream in your hard times.

You're allowed to weep in your hard times.

You're allowed to grumble in your hard times.

You're allowed to sit down in your hard times.

You're allowed to rest in your hard times.

You're allowed to hide in your hard times.

You're allowed to contemplate in your hard times.

But, you're not allowed to give up.

The moment you'll give up in your life, the very moment you'll lose everything in your life.

Never give!

Always try to stand up!

8

If you fall down in your first attempt, it's okay.

Accept it!

If you fall down in your second attempt, it's okay.

Accept it!

If you fall down in your third attempt, it's okay.

Accept it!

……………...

………………

Even if you fall down in your seventh attempt, it's okay.

Accept it!

But, stand up in your eighth attempt.

You'll never know what will happen in your life.

Everything is mystery in your life.

Sometimes the bad things will happen in your life, one after another.

You'll never stop them.

But ***these bad things will put you directly on the path of the best things in your life.***

॰***॰

Almighty God doesn't want to make you weak; but He wants to make you strong.

He doesn't want to make you mediocre; but He wants to make you powerful.

He doesn't want to make you a poor, but He wants to make you a rich.

He doesn't want to make you a coward, but He wants to make you a brave.

He doesn't want to make you a worthless; but He wants to make you a worthy.

That's why He gives you the hardest challenge in your life.

He gives you the toughest situation in your life.

He gives you the hardest battle in your life.

Always remember that 'Almighty God gives the hardest battle to His strongest soldier.

He has chosen you His strongest soldier.'

⌣***⌣

The easiest way in your life is to quit, but whenever you feel like quitting, then ask yourself why you started.

Always remember that *'Winners never quit. Only losers quit before the race.'*

꙰***꙰

You can only achieve the best things when you face the hardest things in your life.

You can only touch the highest summit when you climb the hardest climb in your life.

You can live the good life when you come across the hardest times in your life.

Always remember that *'the biggest results always demand the biggest sacrifice from you.'*

〜***〜

When you face the hard times in your life, then you must tell yourself, "I am going to make it, no matter whatsoever happens to me."

Repeat the same sentence again and again until it will not inject into your mind, body and soul.

Self-affirm yourself, *"I am going to make it, no matter whatsoever happens to me...."*

ᵔ***ᵔ

Don't worry about your hard times.

Since, your hard times are the best time to build your determination and inner strength.

Don't worry about your hard times.

Since, your hard times help you to discover the hidden potential of your determination and inner strength.

Don't worry about your hard times.

Since, ***your hard times are the best time to build the foundation of your energy and power.***

~***~

Your hard times make you weak.

But, never lose your hope.

Come out with strong mindset.

Your hard times make you depressed.

But, never lose your hope.

Come out with new zest and enthusiasm.

Your hard times make you hopeless and hapless.

But, never lose your hope.

Come out with new energy and strength.

Your hard times give you infinite disappointments.

But never lose your hope.

Come out with your infinite persistence.

᷍***᷍

Your hard times are the best time to check your true friends.

Your hard times are the best time to know your worst enemy.

Your hard times are the best time to discover your well wishers.

Your hard times are the best time to find out your true beloved ones.

Since, ***your hard times are the best time to see the true colors of everyone.***

৴***৲

17

Don't worry about your hard times.

But, greet them with your open arms.

Face them with your full might.

Only you can fight back against your hard times.

Nobody can help you.

Only you can help yourself.

Don't wait for anybody.

You've to stand for yourself.

As the storms make trees take deeper roots, in the same fashion the hardest times of your life make you stronger and powerful.

～***～

Do you want to discover the infinite source of your
energy and power?

Do you want to discover your infinite potential?

Do you want to discover your hidden talents and skills?

Do you want to discover your inner-self?

Do you want to discover your true-identity?

If your answers are big 'YES,'

Then, everything will be revealed to you when you face
the hardest times of your life.

***It's during the hardest times when the real hero
within you will be discovered.***

Who is the real treasure in your hard times?

Your real treasure is the people who stayed with you during your hard times.

Your real treasure is the people who helped you during your hard times.

Your real treasure is the people who guided you during your hard times.

Your real treasure is the people who led you during your hard times.

Your real treasure is the people who stood with you during your hard times.

᠊***᠊

"I will give up………..!"

"I will quit……….!"

"I can't stand anymore…………!"

"I don't see any hope………..!"

"It's too tough………..!"

"I can't fight anymore………..!"

These above sentences are the most destructive sentences during your hard times.

Therefore, never ever utter these sentences in your wildest dream.

But, replace these sentences with:

"I will never give up………….!"

"I will never quit………..!"

"I can stand up………….!"

"I can see new hope………..!"

"It's easy………..!"

"I can fight back………..!"

You're the only fighter in the battle of your hard times.

~***~

Don't get discouraged during your hard times.

Motivate yourself!

Encourage yourself!

You're the only one who can motivate and encourage yourself.

You've to act your own power booster.

Don't lose your hope.

Just wait with patient.

Your hard times will pass.

∽***∽

Your hard times are the best time to sharpen your skills and talents.

Take your hard times as your new challenge.

Take your hard times as your new opportunities.

Take your hard times as your new battle.

Take your hard times as your new beginning.

Take your hard times as your blessings in disguise.

Face them and work hard.

You'll definitely come out with the flying colors.

ᔕ***ᔆ

Do you ever see the blooming flower losing its beauty and fragrance during hot summer season; during cold freezing winter season; during windy and rainy season; and during windy and stormy season?

No!

The flower never loses its beauty and fragrance during its hard times.

But, it always keeps its beautiful smile alive.

What about you?

Never ever allow your smile to wither during your hard times.

But, always keep it on your face alive.

There is a great strength in your smile.

～***～

You never win any battle in your first attempt.

You never win any battle in your second attempt.

You never win any battle in your third attempt.

You never win any battle in your fourth attempt.

But, you've to fight again and again, and countless numbers of times, until you'll not witness your greatest triumph.

In the similar manner, your hard times are.

You've to fight against the hard times again and again in your life....

You've to always prepare yourself for your hard times....

Because, you never know when your hard times will knock at your door steps....

Prepare your mind for your hard times....

Prepare your heart for your hard times....

Prepare your body for your hard times...

Prepare your soul for your hard times....

Prepare your actions for your hard times....

Don't wait for anything....

Just prepare yourself today....

Just prepare yourself now....

Just prepare yourself from this very moment....

Your hard times never inform you before it hits in your life....

༈***༈

Your life is like a big battlefield.

In this battlefield of your life, you'll come across many battles one after another.

Some battles are very tough and challenging.

Some battles are nail-biting.

But don't afraid of these battles of your life.

Be brave and fight like a true-soldier.

You're the fighter of your own life.

Never give up!

You've every right to win these battles of your life.

⸜***⸝

You never stop the hard times of your life.

And at the same time, you never stop the good times of your life.

Both the good times and hard times are like the two sides of a coin.

These are like the cycle of your life.

They come one after another.

If you're facing your hard times, then your good times are not far behind of you.

As your bad times will pass, as your good times will arrive.

You've to just wait and keep your patience.

⌇***⌇

Never allow your dreams to shatter during your hard times.

Always keep your dreams alive, no matter whatsoever happens in your life.

Keep the burning lamp of your dreams.

Never allow your dreams to put off.

Without dreams, your life is just like a blank paper.

Your dreams are like the roadmap of your life.

You'll only survive in this world, because you know how to dream in your life.

A life without dreams is like a ship without an anchor.

Always remember that ***'Only a great dreamer can rule this world.'***

The hard times are not for a weak and a coward man.

But, the hard times are for a strong and a brave man.

Are you a weak man or a strong man?

Are you a coward or a brave?

Ask yourself!

And figure out yourself....

Then move ahead in your life....

No hard times ever dare to stop you in the path of your life.

You'll always glimpse your bright future....

﹁***﹁

If you're positive, you'll always see good things in your hard times.

If you're positive, you'll always see new opportunity in your hard times.

If you're positive, you'll know how to handle yourself in your hard times.

If you're positive, you'll know how to face your hard times.

If you're positive, you'll know the differences between the hard times and the good times of your life.

If you're positive, you'll know your hard times will come to the end one day.

Then your good times will be resumed.

$\backsim$***$\backsim$

If you want an easy work,

Then you'll never find the great things in your life.

It's only the difficult work that enriches your life.

If you want an easy job,

Then you'll never find the excellence in your life.

It's only the tough job that excels you in your life.

If you want an easy way,

Then you'll never find the glory in your life.

It's only the tricky way that helps you to discover your glorious destination.

If you want the easy things,

Then you'll never relish the beauty of your life.

It's only the tough things that unfold the wonders of your life.

If you want an easy life,

Then you'll never discover the infinite treasures of your life.

It's only the hard life that unearths the Treasure Island of your life.

◞***◞

Do you want to grow in your life?

Do you want to develop in your life?

Do you want to progress in your life?

Do you want to fulfill your dreams in your life?

Do you want to scale the highest summit in your life?

Do you want to achieve something great in your life?

If your answer is 'YES',

Then, don't afraid of hard times of your life.

Embrace the hard times of your life.

Since, without facing your hard times, you never fulfill anything in your life.

Make friendship with your hard times.

Do you want to check your energy?

Do you want to check your power?

Do you want to check your strength?

Do you want to check your caliber?

Do you want to check your inner-potential?

Do you want to check your skills and talents?

Do you want to check your self-believe?

Do you want to check your self-confidence?

Do you want to check your patience?

Do you want to check your persistence?

Then, ***your hard times are the best time to check your strong character.***

It's only the hard times that help you to build your strong personality.

34

Do you know why the hard times are placed in your way?

The hard times are placed in your way, not to give you disgrace and setbacks, but to encourage you, and to become a brave, so that you can dig out the hidden gems in it.

Nothing is available for free of cost in this world.

You've to go through the hard times in order to get the gems of your life.

~***~

The journey of a butterfly is not an easy....

When it is a caterpillar inside the cocoon; it has to come across the hard times, full of darkness, full of stresses and disgrace....

But the poor little thing doesn't give up....

It fights every moment, tirelessly, until its little wings don't come out from the sticky gel....

In the similar way, ***the journey of your life is not an easy...***

You, too, have to come across the hard times, full of difficulties, full of challenges....until you wouldn't reach to your ultimate goal.....

◞***◟

After every dark night, the bright sun will shine again....

This is the law of nature.

You've to accept it!

After every dry autumn season, the beautiful spring season will arrive again....

This is the law of nature.

You've to accept it!

After the hard times in your life, the good times in your life will come again....

This is the law of life.

You've to accept it!

Always remember that **'even the darkest clouds have the sun behind them.'**

‿***‿

The tiny little seed knows that her dream to become the most beautiful plant is not an easy.....

In order to fulfill its dream into reality, it has to be dropped in the dirt, covered in darkness, and struggle to reach the light....

Then only it will grow into a beautiful plant and come out from the dark world....

What about you?

Do you aware of your dreams?

Do you know how to fulfill your dreams into reality?

Do you know how many struggles you'll have to face?

Are you ready to prepare yourself?

The tiny little seed knows that her dream to become the most beautiful plant is not an easy.....

Do you know about yourself?

Until you'll not witness your failure, you don't know the importance of your success.

Until you'll not fall down, you don't know the importance of bounce back.

Until you'll not lose, you don't know the importance of gaining.

Until you'll not see your hardship, you don't know the importance of your happiness.

Until you'll not survive in your hard times, you don't know the importance of your good times.

༄***༄

What is the biggest weapon to fight against the hard times of your life?

Your self-believe is the biggest weapon to fight against the hard times of your life.

If you've self-believe, you can do anything in your life.

Nothing is impossible for you.

You can win your lost battle.

You can regain your lost wealth.

You can turn your failure into your grand success.

You can rebuild your lost glory.

It always depends upon you how to act during your hard times.

Either you act in a positive way or in a negative way.

You've to make your own choice.

If you act in a positive way, you'll always see your new opportunities.

If you act in a negative way, you'll always see your downfall and failure.

It always depends upon you how to react during your hard times.

Either you react strongly or weakly.

You've to make your own choice.

If you react strongly, you'll always become a winner.

If you react weakly, you'll always become a loser.

It always depends upon you how to respond during your hard times.

Either you respond bravely or cowardly.

You've to make your own choice.

If you respond bravely, you'll become successful in your life.

If you respond cowardly, you'll always live your life in utter darkness and doom.

~***~

If you get the irresistible criticism in your life, be patient and tough; someday this criticism will be useful to you.

If you face the worst situation in your life, be patient and tough; someday this situation will be useful to you.

If you're wounded in your life, be patient and tough; someday this wound will be useful to you.

If you go through the hardest pain in your life, be patient and tough; someday this pain will be useful to you.

〜***〜

Let the hard times twist you harder and harder,

But don't give up!

In the end you will come out cleaner than ever before.

Let the hard times turn you harder and harder,

But don't give up!

In the end you will come out brighter than ever before.

Let the hard times knock you harder and harder,

But don't give up!

In the end you will come out brighter than ever before.

〜***〜

⌣***⌣

Never ever give up your great ideas, no matter how many hard times attack on your life.

You're bound to fulfill your great ideas.

Never ever give up your great dreams, no matter how many hard times strike in your life.

You're bound to fulfill your greatest dreams.

Never ever give up your great goals of your life, no matter how many hard times knock in your life.

You're bound to fulfill your greatest goals.

Never ever give up your great objectives of your life, no matter how many hard times hit in your life.

You're bound to fulfill your greatest objectives.

Never ever give up your great purposes of your life, no matter how many hard times bombarded in your life.

You're bound to fulfill your greatest purposes.

⌣***⌣

ᔐ***ᔑ

Whatever life gives you, even if it hurts you,

Accept it!

Just be strong.

Act like you're okay.

But, never run away…..

Whatever life gives you, even if it discourages you,

Accept it!

Just be strong.

Act like you're okay.

But, never run away…..

Whatever life gives you, even if it shatters you down,

Accept it!

Just be strong,

Act like you're okay.

But, never run away…..

Always remember that **'the strong walls shake, but never collapse.'**

ᔐ***ᔑ

If you are going through unhappiness and sad, have faith that happiness and joy are on the way.

If you are going through downfall and failure, have faith that success and glory are on the way.

If you are going through hard times, have faith that good times are on the way.

~***~

Every struggle in your life has shaped you into the person you are today.

So, be thankful for the struggle.

It can only make you stronger.

Every obstacle in your life has shaped you into the person you are today.

So, be thankful for the obstacle.

It can only make you stronger.

Every challenge in your life has shaped you into the person you are today.

So, be thankful for the challenge.

It can only make you stronger.

Every battle in your life has shaped you into the person you are today.

So, be thankful for the battle.

It can only make you stronger.

The hard times in your life has shaped you into the person you are today.

So, be thankful for the hard times.

They can only make you stronger.

⌇***⌇

If you're rejected from something good, don't shed your precious tears.

But, think and act in a positive way.

Keep the burning lamp of your hope alive.

Be patient.

Wait for your good time…..

One day, the time will arrive in your life, when you realize yourself that you're actually not rejected from the good things,

But, you're re-directed to something better.

Never wait for the easy ways in your life…..

The more difficult is the ways; more joy and happiness are waiting for you…

Never wait for the easy roads in your life….

The more difficult is the roads; the most beautiful destinations are waiting for you…

Never wait for the easy life…..

The more difficult is the life, the more comfortable and contentment is waiting for you….

Always remember that *'if you want to reach to the beautiful destinations in your life, you've to travel the difficult roads…..'*

ᔖ***ᔖ

In your hard times,

Nobody will wipe out your flowing tears…..

You'll never find anyone…..

You've to wipe out your own flowing tears.

In your hard times,

Nobody will heal your bleeding wounds….

You'll never find anyone…..

You've to heal your own bleeding wounds.

In your hard times,

Nobody will hold your collapsing body…..

You'll never find anyone…..

You've to hold your own collapsing body.

In your hard times,

Nobody will pour the dose of love and compassion to
your drying feelings and emotions…..

You'll never find anyone…..

You've to pour the dose of love and compassion to your own drying feelings and emotions.

In your hard times,

Nobody will boost up your dying moral and spirit.....

You'll never find anyone....

You've to boost up your own dying moral and spirit.

*~***~*

50

Are you worried about your hard times?

If you're worried about your hard times, you can't survive anymore in this world.

Sooner or later, you'll fall down....

You'll harm yourself.

Are you afraid of your hard times?

If you're afraid of your hard times, you can't stand anymore in this world.

Sooner or later, you'll collapse....

You'll kill yourself.

Don't fear your hard times.

The hard times are like the roaring thunderstorms.

They make a lot of deafening noises.

But, they do little harm.

They will pass.....

◡***◡

Without your hard times, you'll never explore the blessings of your life…

Without your hard times, you'll never know the real meaning of your life….

Without your hard times, you'll never know the true purpose of your life….

Without your hard times, you'll never discover your true identity.

Therefore, always greet your hard times…..

Always pay your greatest gratitude…..

Face them just like you're meeting your best comrade…

Hug them!

Love them!

Since, ***there is a great hand in your hard times to rebuild you from an ordinary person to an extraordinary person.***

About the author:

Birister Sharma is a full time author. He is also an avid reader. He loves reading, writing, and motivation. He has penned down dozens of self-help motivational books and novels so far.

You may contact him @ birister2007@gmail.com